PRESENTS

ALL ABOUT
ULTIMATE WARRIOR
FACT BOOK

BY LARRY HUMBER

CHECKERBOARD PRESS
NEW YORK

THE ULTIMATE WARRIOR—the supreme

fighting force—burst onto the scene of the WWF a few years ago. No one knows where he came from.

His story is told in the ring. Already he has won two titles: the World Wrestling Federation Championship and the Intercontinental Championship.

Let's look at the man and his many battles...

BACKGROUND STUFF

✳ The Warrior is no 99-pound weakling. He weighs in at 275 pounds, and there's not an ounce of fat on him.

✳ Not only do we not know where the Warrior calls home, but his date of birth is also a mystery.

✳ According to the Warrior, warriors must always be ready for battle. "If you're not, you're finished," he says.

✳ The Warrior likes to hoist his beaten foes high above his head and then drop them like a ton of bricks. He calls that his gorilla press slam.

✴ The Warrior is also known for his big splash, which is just what it sounds like. He throws his whole weight onto his fallen opponents.

THE FIRST TITLE

✸ The Warrior's first big test was at *SummerSlam '88,* where he fought the Honky Tonk Man for the Intercontinental Title.

✸ The Warrior was taking the place of another wrestler at *SummerSlam '88.* Brutus "The Barber" Beefcake was supposed to fight Honky but could not because of an injury.

✸ Warrior didn't hesitate. He jumped the Honky Tonk Man even before he could remove his jewel-covered outfit.

✳ Warrior used a vicious clothesline to end the bout, leaving Honky Tonk out to dry and out of the Intercontinental Belt.

✳ Honky was very upset. He said that the bell had never sounded. But nobody listened to him.

POSEDOWN

✳ The Warrior has the build of a champion. At the *Royal Rumble* in 1989 he took part in a special contest to determine who had the best body in the WWF.

✳ The contest—called the Super Posedown—matched the Warrior against Ravishing Rick Rude.

✸ The judging was done by the fans attending the *Rumble.*

✸ When it looked as if the Warrior had won, Rude blew his top. He clubbed the Warrior with an exercise bar and choked him.

✸ The Warrior was knocked out. When he came to, he went wild. He began lashing out at anyone who came near him.

WRESTLEMANIA V

✳ Warrior was so mad at Rude that he offered him a title match at *WrestleMania V.* Would the Warrior keep his Intercontinental Championship?

✳ Rude showed that he wasn't done with his dirty tricks by jumping the Warrior.

✳ Rude took control early in the match, but Warrior wasn't finished. He clotheslined Rude right out of the ring.

✸ Rude's manager—wily Bobby "The Brain" Heenan—couldn't stand to see his man lose. He tripped the Warrior and held on to his leg, which allowed Rude to pin him.

✸ Warrior lost his belt, but he would soon have it back. He battered and bashed Rude at *SummerSlam '89* to take the title again.

WORDS OF WARRIOR

✳ Warrior is a man of few words, so when he talks, you'd better listen!

* Warrior says that the best defense is a good offense.

* Warrior is not one to hold anything back. However, he says a man should never ever hit a woman—even one as sneaky as Sensational Sherri.

✴ Warrior dedicates his triumphs in the ring to the great fighting men of the past. "I do them homage in battle," he says.

✴ When Warrior can't find the words to express himself, he just growls and beats his mighty chest.

HISTORY LESSONS

❋ Warrior is often compared with the great warriors of history. Their lives were spent on the field of battle.

❋ One of the Warrior's favorite fighting men is the legendary Achilles. He was the Trojan War hero who had only one weak spot—his heel.

❋ Warrior also admires Genghis Khan, a Mongol conqueror of years gone by.

* Alexander the Great is another of the Warrior's heroes. He conquered the fabled Persian Empire.

* Among the qualities the Warrior shares with his heroes is his fearlessness. Like them, he is afraid of nothing.

THE EYE OF THE HULKSTER

✳ Warrior finally got his chance against the immortal Hulk Hogan at *WrestleMania VI*. Hulk was the holder of the WWF Championship. Warrior was the Intercontinental Champion.

✳ The bout began with a test of strength. Neither man was able to show up the other.

✳ Both were nearly knocked out later in the contest when they clotheslined each other to the canvas.

✳ Warrior finally pinned the Hulkster. A true champion, Hulk handed Warrior his belt, raised his arm, and hugged him.

✳ WWF President Jack Tunney made the Warrior give up his other belt when he won the WWF Championship. Tunney also ruled that Warrior and Hulk could not fight again for fear that they would do each other "torturous injury."

THE SNEAKY SERGEANT

✳ Warrior held the WWF Championship until *Royal Rumble* in 1991. He should have known better than to take on Sgt. Slaughter—the Sarge is a real skunk.

✳ Slaughter was joined in the ring by his commanding officer, General Adnan. He is not to be trusted either.

✴ Slaughter had yet another helper—Macho King Randy Savage. Savage didn't sit still for long. He smashed Warrior across the back with some TV equipment. Later he hit him over the head with his scepter.

✴ Thanks to Savage's dirty work, Slaughter pinned the Warrior. But the Sarge would get his soon after. Hulk Hogan pounded him at *WrestleMania VII*.

QUITTING TIME

✸ The Warrior wanted to get back at Savage. He challenged him to a Career Match at *WrestleMania VII.*

✸ Warrior wanted to end Savage's career once and for all. So he made Savage agree that the loser would have to retire from the WWF.

* Savage nearly pinned him on several occasions, but the Warrior kicked out at the last moment.

* In the end, Warrior got the better of Savage. Victorious, he stood with his arms raised, a foot on Savage's chest.

* When Warrior left, Savage was joined by his former manager, Miss Elizabeth, who showed her affection for the Macho King.

✳ As for the Warrior, he would return to fight another day.